This sp[...]

BOOK OF THANKS

belongs to—

_____

Draw a picture of yourself

TODAY I AM
THANKFUL FOR ....

thank you ♥ _____

thank you ♥ _____

thank you ♥ _____

Write about or draw your
FAVOURITE part of the day

TODAY I AM
THANKFUL FOR ....

thank you ♥ _____

thank you ♥ _____

thank you ♥ _____

Write about or draw your
FAVOURITE part of the day

TODAY I AM
THANKFUL FOR ....

thank
you ♥ _____

thank
you ♥ _____

thank
you ♥ _____

Write about or draw your
FAVOURITE part of the day

TODAY I AM THANKFUL FOR ....

thank you ♥ _____

thank you ♥ _____

thank you ♥ _____

Write about or draw your
FAVOURITE part of the day

TODAY I AM
THANKFUL FOR ....

thank you ♥ _____

thank you ♥ _____

thank you ♥ _____

Write about or draw your
FAVOURITE part of the day

I AM THANKFUL

for my family

TODAY I AM
THANKFUL FOR ....

♥ ❤ ♥ ❤ ♥ ❤ ♥ ❤

thank you ♥ _____

thank you ♥ _____

thank you ♥ _____

Write about or draw your
FAVOURITE part of the day

TODAY I AM THANKFUL FOR ....
♥•♥•♥•♥•♥•♥•♥

thank you♥ _____

thank you♥ _____

thank you♥ _____

Write about or draw your
FAVOURITE part of the day

TODAY I AM THANKFUL FOR ....

♥ ♥ ♥ ♥ ♥ ♥ ♥ ♥ ♥

thank you ♥ _____

thank you ♥ _____

thank you ♥ _____

Write about or draw your
FAVOURITE part of the day

TODAY I AM THANKFUL FOR ....

thank you ♥ _____

thank you ♥ _____

thank you ♥ _____

Write about or draw your FAVOURITE part of the day

TODAY I AM THANKFUL FOR ....

thank you ♥ _____

thank you ♥ _____

thank you ♥ _____

Write about or draw your FAVOURITE part of the day

TODAY I AM THANKFUL FOR ....

thank you ♥ _____

thank you ♥ _____

thank you ♥ _____

Write about or draw your
FAVOURITE part of the day

TODAY I AM THANKFUL FOR ....

thank you ♥ _____

thank you ♥ _____

thank you ♥ _____

Write about or draw your
FAVOURITE part of the day

TODAY I AM THANKFUL FOR ....

thank you ♥ _____

thank you ♥ _____

thank you ♥ _____

Write about or draw your FAVOURITE part of the day

TODAY I AM
THANKFUL FOR ....
♥ ♥ ♥ ♥

thank you ♥ _____

thank you ♥ _____

thank you ♥ _____

Write about or draw your
FAVOURITE part of the day

I AM THANKFUL

that I remember how
lucky I am

TODAY I AM
THANKFUL FOR ....

thank you ♥ _____

thank you ♥ _____

thank you ♥ _____

Write about or draw your
FAVOURITE part of the day

TODAY I AM
THANKFUL FOR ....
♥ ♥ ♥ ♥ ♥ ♥ ♥ ♥ ♥

thank you ♥ _____

thank you ♥ _____

thank you ♥ _____

Write about or draw your
FAVOURITE part of the day

TODAY I AM
THANKFUL FOR ....

thank you ♥ _____

thank you ♥ _____

thank you ♥ _____

Write about or draw your
FAVOURITE part of the day

TODAY I AM THANKFUL FOR ....

thank you ♥ _____

thank you ♥ _____

thank you ♥ _____

Write about or draw your
FAVOURITE part of the day

TODAY I AM
THANKFUL FOR ....

thank you ♥ _____

thank you ♥ _____

thank you ♥_____

Write about or draw your
FAVOURITE part of the day

TODAY I AM THANKFUL FOR ....

thank you ♥ _____

thank you ♥ _____

thank you ♥

Write about or draw your FAVOURITE part of the day

TODAY I AM
THANKFUL FOR ....

thank you ♥ _____

thank you ♥ _____

thank you ♥ _____

Write about or draw your
FAVOURITE part of the day

I AM THANKFUL

that I am loved

TODAY I AM
THANKFUL FOR ....

thank you ♥ _____

thank you ♥ _____

thank you ♥ _____

Write about or draw your
FAVOURITE part of the day

TODAY I AM
THANKFUL FOR ....

thank you ♥ _____

thank you ♥ _____

thank you ♥ _____

Write about or draw your FAVOURITE part of the day

TODAY I AM
THANKFUL FOR ....

thank you ♥ ———————————————————

thank you ♥ ———————————————————

thank you ♥ ———————————————————

Write about or draw your
FAVOURITE part of the day

TODAY I AM THANKFUL FOR ....

thank you ♥ _____

thank you ♥ _____

thank you ♥ _____

Write about or draw your
FAVOURITE part of the day

TODAY I AM THANKFUL FOR ....

thank you ♥ _____

thank you ♥ _____

thank you ♥ _____

Write about or draw your
FAVOURITE part of the day

TODAY I AM
THANKFUL FOR ....

thank you ♥ _____

thank you ♥ _____

thank you ♥ _____

Write about or draw your
FAVOURITE part of the day

TODAY I AM THANKFUL FOR ....

♥ ♥ ♥ ♥ ♥

thank you ♥ _____

thank you ♥ _____

thank you ♥ _____

Write about or draw your
FAVOURITE part of the day

TODAY I AM
THANKFUL FOR ....

thank you ♥ _____

thank you ♥ _____

thank you ♥ _____

Write about or draw your
FAVOURITE part of the day

I AM THANKFUL

for the happiness I share

TODAY I AM THANKFUL FOR ....

thank you ♥ _____

thank you ♥ _____

thank you ♥ _____

Write about or draw your FAVOURITE part of the day

TODAY I AM THANKFUL FOR ....

thank you ♥ _____

thank you ♥ _____

thank you ♥ _____

Write about or draw your FAVOURITE part of the day

TODAY I AM THANKFUL FOR ....

thank you ♥ _____

thank you ♥ _____

thank you ♥ _____

Write about or draw your
FAVOURITE part of the day

TODAY I AM THANKFUL FOR ....

thank you ♥ _____

thank you ♥ _____

thank you ♥ _____

Write about or draw your FAVOURITE part of the day

TODAY I AM
THANKFUL FOR ....

thank you ♥ _____

thank you ♥ _____

thank you ♥ _____

Write about or draw your
FAVOURITE part of the day

TODAY I AM THANKFUL FOR ....

thank you ♥ _____

thank you ♥ _____

thank you ♥ _____

Write about or draw your FAVOURITE part of the day

TODAY I AM THANKFUL FOR ....

♥ ♥ ♥ ♥ ♥ ♥ ♥

thank you ♥ _____

thank you ♥ _____

thank you ♥ _____

Write about or draw your
FAVOURITE part of the day

TODAY I AM
THANKFUL FOR ....

thank you ♥ _____

thank you ♥ _____

thank you ♥ _____

Write about or draw your
FAVOURITE part of the day

TODAY I AM
THANKFUL FOR ....

thank you ♥ _____

thank you ♥ _____

thank you ♥ _____

Write about or draw your
FAVOURITE part of the day

I AM THANKFUL

that I have a home

TODAY I AM THANKFUL FOR ....

thank you ♥ _____

thank you ♥ _____

thank you ♥ _____

Write about or draw your FAVOURITE part of the day

TODAY I AM THANKFUL FOR ....

thank you ♥ _____

thank you ♥ _____

thank you ♥ _____

Write about or draw your
FAVOURITE part of the day

TODAY I AM
THANKFUL FOR ....
♥ ♥ ♥ ♥ ♥ ♥ ♥

thank you ♥ _____

thank you ♥ _____

thank you ♥ _____

Write about or draw your
FAVOURITE part of the day

TODAY I AM THANKFUL FOR ....
♥ ♥ ♥ ♥ ♥ ♥ ♥

thank you ♥ _____

thank you ♥ _____

thank you ♥ _____

Write about or draw your
FAVOURITE part of the day

TODAY I AM THANKFUL FOR ....

hank you ♥ _____

hank you ♥ _____

hank you ♥ _____

Write about or draw your
FAVOURITE part of the day

TODAY I AM THANKFUL FOR ....

thank you ♥ _____

thank you ♥ _____

thank you ♥ _____

Write about or draw your
FAVOURITE part of the day

TODAY I AM
THANKFUL FOR ....

thank you ♥ _____

thank you ♥ _____

thank you ♥ _____

Write about or draw your
FAVOURITE part of the day

TODAY I AM THANKFUL FOR ....

thank you ♥ _____

thank you ♥ _____

thank you ♥ _____

Write about or draw your
FAVOURITE part of the day

TODAY I AM THANKFUL FOR ....

thank you ♥ _____

thank you ♥ _____

thank you ♥ _____

Write about or draw your FAVOURITE part of the day

I AM THANKFUL

for being me and shining bright

TODAY I AM THANKFUL FOR ....

thank you ♥ _____

thank you ♥ _____

thank you ♥ _____

Write about or draw your FAVOURITE part of the day

TODAY I AM THANKFUL FOR ....

thank you ♥ _____

thank you ♥ _____

thank you ♥ _____

Write about or draw your FAVOURITE part of the day

TODAY I AM THANKFUL FOR ....

thank you ♥ _____

thank you ♥ _____

thank you ♥ _____

Write about or draw your FAVOURITE part of the day

TODAY I AM
THANKFUL FOR ....

thank you ♥ _____

thank you ♥ _____

thank you ♥ _____

Write about or draw your
FAVOURITE part of the day

TODAY I AM
THANKFUL FOR ....

thank
you ♥ _____

thank
you ♥ _____

thank
you ♥ _____

Write about or draw your
FAVOURITE part of the day

TODAY I AM THANKFUL FOR ....

thank you ♥ _____

thank you ♥ _____

thank you ♥ _____

Write about or draw your FAVOURITE part of the day

TODAY I AM
THANKFUL FOR ....

thank you ♥ _____

thank you ♥ _____

thank you ♥ _____

Write about or draw your
FAVOURITE part of the day

TODAY I AM
THANKFUL FOR ....

thank you ♥ _____

thank you ♥ _____

thank you ♥ _____

Write about or draw your
FAVOURITE part of the day

TODAY I AM
THANKFUL FOR ....

thank you ♥ _____

thank you ♥ _____

thank you ♥ _____

Write about or draw your
FAVOURITE part of the day

TODAY I AM THANKFUL FOR ....

thank you ♥—————————————————————

thank you ♥—————————————————————

thank you ♥—————————————————————

Write about or draw your FAVOURITE part of the day

TODAY I AM
THANKFUL FOR ....

thank
you ♥ _____

thank
you ♥ _____

thank
you ♥

Write about or draw your
FAVOURITE part of the day

TODAY I AM THANKFUL FOR ....

thank you ♥ ———————————————

thank you ♥ ———————————————

thank you ♥ ———————————————

Write about or draw your FAVOURITE part of the day

TODAY I AM
THANKFUL FOR ....

thank you ♥ _____

thank you ♥ _____

thank you ♥ _____

Write about or draw your
FAVOURITE part of the day

I AM THANKFUL

for everyone who loves me,
near and far

TODAY I AM
THANKFUL FOR ....

thank
you ♥ _____

thank
you ♥ _____

thank
you ♥ _____

Write about or draw your
FAVOURITE part of the day

TODAY I AM
THANKFUL FOR ....

thank you ♥ _____

thank you ♥ _____

thank you ♥ _____

Write about or draw your
FAVOURITE part of the day

TODAY I AM THANKFUL FOR ....

thank you ♥ _____

thank you ♥ _____

thank you ♥ _____

Write about or draw your FAVOURITE part of the day

TODAY I AM
THANKFUL FOR ....

thank you ♥ _____

thank you ♥ _____

thank you ♥ _____

Write about or draw your
FAVOURITE part of the day

TODAY I AM THANKFUL FOR ....

♥ ♥ ♥ ♥ ♥ ♥ ♥ ♥ ♥

thank you ♥ _____

thank you ♥ _____

thank you ♥ _____

Write about or draw your FAVOURITE part of the day

TODAY I AM THANKFUL FOR ....

thank you ♥ _____

thank you ♥ _____

thank you ♥ _____

Write about or draw your FAVOURITE part of the day

TODAY I AM THANKFUL FOR ....

thank you ♥ _____

thank you ♥ _____

thank you ♥ _____

Write about or draw your FAVOURITE part of the day

I AM THANKFUL

for sunrises

TODAY I AM THANKFUL FOR ....

♥ ♥ ♥ ♥ ♥ ♥ ♥

thank you ♥ _____

thank you ♥ _____

thank you ♥ _____

Write about or draw your
FAVOURITE part of the day

TODAY I AM THANKFUL FOR ....

thank you ♥ ———————————————

thank you ♥ ———————————————

thank you ♥ ———————————————

Write about or draw your FAVOURITE part of the day

TODAY I AM
THANKFUL FOR ....

thank you ♥ _____

thank you ♥ _____

thank you ♥ _____

Write about or draw your FAVOURITE part of the day

TODAY I AM THANKFUL FOR ....

thank you ♥ _____

thank you ♥ _____

thank you ♥ _____

Write about or draw your FAVOURITE part of the day

TODAY I AM THANKFUL FOR ....

thank you ♥ _____

thank you ♥ _____

thank you ♥ _____

Write about or draw your FAVOURITE part of the day

TODAY I AM
THANKFUL FOR ....

thank you ♥ _____

thank you ♥ _____

thank you ♥ _____

Write about or draw your
FAVOURITE part of the day

TODAY I AM
THANKFUL FOR ....

thank you 🖤 _____

thank you 🖤 _____

thank you 🖤 _____

Write about or draw your
FAVOURITE part of the day

I AM THANKFUL

for times to rest and relax

TODAY I AM THANKFUL FOR ....

thank you ♥ _____

thank you ♥ _____

thank you ♥ _____

Write about or draw your
FAVOURITE part of the day

TODAY I AM THANKFUL FOR ....

♥ ♥ ♥ ♥

thank you ♥ _____

thank you ♥ _____

thank you ♥ _____

Write about or draw your FAVOURITE part of the day

TODAY I AM THANKFUL FOR ....

thank you ♥ _____

thank you ♥ _____

thank you ♥ _____

Write about or draw your FAVOURITE part of the day

TODAY I AM THANKFUL FOR ....

thank you ♥ _____

thank you ♥ _____

thank you ♥

Write about or draw your FAVOURITE part of the day

TODAY I AM
THANKFUL FOR ...

thank
you ♥ _____

thank
you ♥ _____

thank
you ♥

Write about or draw your
FAVOURITE part of the day

TODAY I AM THANKFUL FOR ....

thank you ♥ _____

thank you ♥ _____

thank you ♥ _____

Write about or draw your
FAVOURITE part of the day

I AM THANKFUL

for hugs

TODAY I AM THANKFUL FOR ....

thank you ♥ _____

thank you ♥ _____

thank you ♥ _____

Write about or draw your
FAVOURITE part of the day

TODAY I AM
THANKFUL FOR ....

thank you ♥ _____

thank you ♥ _____

thank you ♥ _____

Write about or draw your
FAVOURITE part of the day

TODAY I AM THANKFUL FOR ....

thank you ♥ _____

thank you ♥ _____

thank you ♥ _____

Write about or draw your FAVOURITE part of the day

TODAY I AM THANKFUL FOR ....

thank you 🖤 _____

thank you 🖤 _____

thank you 🖤 _____

Write about or draw your FAVOURITE part of the day

TODAY I AM
THANKFUL FOR ....
♥ ♥ ♥ ♥ ♥ ♥ ♥ ♥ ♥

thank you ♥ _____

thank you ♥ _____

thank you ♥ _____

Write about or draw your
FAVOURITE part of the day

TODAY I AM THANKFUL FOR ....

thank you ♥ _____

thank you ♥ _____

thank you ♥ _____

Write about or draw your FAVOURITE part of the day

TODAY I AM THANKFUL FOR ....

thank you ♥ _____

thank you ♥ _____

thank you ♥ _____

Write about or draw your FAVOURITE part of the day

I AM THANKFUL

for magical times

thank you ♥ Vivien Leanne Saunders for the beautiful bear illustrations on the cover and inside the book. They were originally created to illustrate the children's book I wrote called 'A Bear Christmas' which is about being thankful at Christmas, and it was a joy to bring Buddy into a BOOK of THANKS.

thank you ♥ All the incredible children and young people that I have worked with all over the world in the past 30 years. You are always in mind whenever I create anything. And forever in my heart.

thank you ♥ Whoever purchased this book for themselves, a child, young person or a gift. Thank you for your support and spreading the message of gratitude. I am thankful for you.

Jo Bivens MEd, FRSA, FRSPH.

THE CHILDREN'S COACH
International Education Hero of the Year

 www.thechildrenscoach.com   thechildrenscoach

Printed in Great Britain
by Amazon

69349889R00058